The King Of Riddles

The Massive Conundrum Book
For Teens And Adults

Karen J. Bun

there for you! Remember, riddles are for you to have fun, so have fun! Challenge yourself and others and stretch your brain! Trust us, your brain will thank you. If you feel like you are stumped, you can take a deep breath, walk away, and come back or you can even ask for help. Whatever you do, remember to have fun! You may even want to mark the trickiest riddles to try on your friends and family members.

There are plenty of books on this subject on the market, so thanks again for choosing this one! I do not take it for granted that you decided to purchase this book. Every effort was made to ensure it is full of as much useful information as possible. Please enjoy!

Chapter 1: Super Easy Riddles — "What Am I?"

1. Drier, Yet Wetter

   The more it dries, the wetter it becomes. I can be big or small and used on the beach or at home. What am I?

2. 3 Miles Away

   You may try to chase me, but no matter how close you may think you are, I am always about 3 miles away. I can be beautiful, and people like to take my picture. What am I?

3. Single Eye

   I have a single eye, but I cannot see. If you touch me, you may just prick yourself. What am I?

4. Black Water

   I go in the water black and come out red. I am a special treat for many people who love seafood. What am I?

5. Light as a Feather

   The world's strongest man is not able to hold me for more than 300 seconds even though I am like a feather. Please guess what I am.

6. No Water and Cities

I have bodies of water but no water. I have towns and villages but no beings. I even contain long roads, without any cars. Small or big, I can cover the entire world. What am I?

7. Two Legs

I have two legs, but I cannot walk. I can come in different styles and sizes. What am I?

8. Just Like Bacon

Sizzling like scissors, made with a small egg, containing a long spine, without one leg in sight. Peeling like an onion but longer than a shoelace. I can fit in tiny holes. Guess what I am.

9. An Easy Search

I am easy to get into but can be extremely hard to get out of. Some people love me, other people hate me. What am I?

10. Clap and Rumble

I can clap and rumble without any hands. I am loud and sometimes can be scary, but if you hear me, you know the earth will thank me. What am I?

11. Neck and No Head

Neck. Check. No head. Check. Can wear a cap. Check. You need something special to open me. Figure me out.

12. Big Bark

Big bark. No bite. I exist in different species, but without me, you would experience a certain death. Can you tell me what I am?

13. Smooth or Rough Jacket

I can wear a smooth or rough jacket, but I don't wear any pants. You can open me or close me, but many people see my value. What am I?

14. Up and Down

I am in some of the most famous places in the world all throughout history. I am in some people's house. Down and up I go while being stationary. Please tell me what I am.

15. Fly All Day

Lots of countries have me so I exist in a lot of different colors and sizes. I fly all day, but I stay still like a couch potato. Guess what I am if you can.

16. Wet Coat

I am the type of coat that you can only put on when I am wet. You can put on multiple coats and not get hot. Some people even put up a sign to mark my spot. What am I?

17. Unwinnable Bet

If you are a better, you might not like me because I am the type of bet that can never be won. I consist of many parts and even have my own song. What am I?

18. Unwearable Dress

A snail has me on my back, but I am the type of dress that you cannot wear. Men and women both have me, old and young too. Sometimes ghosts live here and living beings too. What am I?

19. Eyes That Cannot See

Blind eyes, a non-functional tongue, and an immortal soul I have. Some people see me in the clouds in the sky. What am I?

20. Serve, But Not Eaten

You can serve me, but you cannot eat me. Some people love me, and others hate me. I am small, fast, and green. What am I?

21. Limbs But Cannot Walk

I exist all over the world. I have over 100 limbs, but I cannot walk. Animals love to play on me and kids too. What am I?

22. Come Down, But Not Up

I can drizzle or pour. If you see me, some people want a jacket before they go out their home's door. Always coming down, I stay down and never return up. Are you smart enough to figure me out?

23. Beat with No Cries

I am white and yellow, the color of light. When you crack me, I will be alright. I get beaten and whipped but never cry. What am I?

24. Travel in One Spot

I consist of many different spaces, some living and some dead. Sometimes I just may be a shape or color, but you need me in order for a letter to be read. Visiting places in the world while remaining in one place, especially the corner. What am I?

25. Catch

I am one of the most feared things in the winter, and even in the summer. You can catch me but cannot throw me. People who have me can sometimes say, "Achoo." What am I?

26. Four Eyes

I look like a square and even have a delta. I have four eyes, but I cannot see. I am the spot of a lot of history. What am I?

27. Eighty-eight keys

I have eighty-eight keys but can't unlock anything. While tinkling and banging, musicians love to hear my name. What am I?

28. Always Coming

I am not the present, but I am being looked forward to. I am always coming, but I never arrive. Some people have their day planned weeks in advance. What am I?

29. Careful, Fragile

Some people love to make me, and sometimes people hate to make me. I get broken without being held. What am I?

30. Round on Both Sides

I am circular on the ends but reach the highest heights in the middle, all while being an important consideration in the politics of the United States of America. What am I?

31. Lose My Head

I am soft, and sometimes I am hard. I lose my head every morning, but it returns to me every night. Sometimes I am made of cotton, and sometimes I am made of feathers. People love to have me in any weather. What am I?

32. Hear, But No Body

I can be loud, or I can be soft. If you have me, you take me for granted. If you don't have me, you wish that you did. If you have ears, you can hear, but if you have fingers, you can't touch me or see me if you have eyes. What am I?

33. Poor and Rich People

There are a lot of people who get mad if they get me as a gift. Poor people have too much of it, but rich people supposedly will benefit from more of me. Eating me is a sure cause of death. Tell me what I am.

34. No Sharing

There is something unique about me. I am special and only a few people should know about me. If I share me, there's no point, and if you have me, no sharing, please. Can you figure out what I am?

35. The More You Take

I can be big or small, but you will need me at some point in your life. The more you take away, the larger I become. Some animals like to call me their home. What am I?

36. Born in the Air

If you are quiet, I am no longer there. I live with no body, experience audio with no ears, and verbalize with no mouth. Oh yeah, I'm birthed in the air. What am I?

37. Millions of Years

I can be white or orange and big or small. I have been here since the beginning of time but caught in an unending cycle of being born every month. What am I?

38. Give It Away

I am a very important part of life. You can keep it only after giving it away to someone else. What is it?

39. Stand on One Leg

Some people love me, and some people hate me, but if you eat me, you should never be dead. Standing straight on one leg with my heart in the same place as my head. Are you able to tell me what I am?

40. You Can Throw Me Away

Squirrels and cows love me. I can be boiled or cooked on the grill. Trash me outside, prepare my innards, and trash my insides when you are finished. Guess what I am.

41. Used for Light

I'm useful for light and solid. No me, and you would feel trapped, but I do not want to be touched. And don't even think of using force. I love being in buildings, and ancient I am if I must say. Most of us use me every day. What am I?

42. Higher Without the Head

I am higher without the head than with it. What am I?

43. If I Drink

I can be loud but start off soft. If you aren't listening, I can be fatal. Partaking of a beverage will cause my death, but partaking in a meal is not dangerous for me. What would you say that I am?

44. Take Away My First Letter

When you erase my first letter, last letter, and middle letter, I still sound the same. I am a five-letter word. What am I?

45. No Bones or Legs

I don't know if it was me or this animal that came first. While I have no legs or bones, if you give me a little heat, I can hurry away. What am I?

46. Tall When Young

My youth equals height and my age equals shortness. I can age fast or slow. If you have no electricity, you'll need me wherever you may go. What am I?

47. Throw Me Away

Pirates love me, and some people have me in their homes. Get rid of me when you want me to be useful. But if you want me to do nothing, bring me back in. What am I?

48. When Water Comes

The water pours, and I appear. The water pours, and I point to the sky. Some people use me to block the very bright sun. What am I?

49. The Maker Doesn't Need Me

If you make me, you will not need me at the moment. If you buy me, you don't even need me for yourself, but if you have to use me, you will never know. What am I?

50. People Need Me to Eat

You often can't have a meal unless you have me because I make your life easy. You need me at mealtime, but I'm not edible. Well, you can, but it wouldn't be very good. What am I?

51. Many Times

You can see me in the snow, and if you need to mark your spot without a compass, I am the way to go. The more you move, the more I trail you. Guess what I am.

52. End of the Rainbow

I am at the end of the colorful rainbow. It doesn't matter how big or small the rainbow is. What am I?

53. Never Ask Questions

I can be musical or just a simple sound. In front of a mansion, I will most likely be found. Questions you will never hear from me, but I get the answers I want. Tell me what I am.

54. No Life

I can be inside or outside. I can be used on lots of different devices. I may be in the background, but you will want to pay attention. Lifeless, I can die. If you don't have me, people can go berserk. I'm sure you know what I am.

55. A Speechless Mouth

With my mouth, I never shout. I can gurgle and murmur without ever stopping. I always jog, more like run, even without any legs. Guess what thing I am.

56. Lots of Memories

Memories are the only things I have because I have no material possessions. I house memories from years ago or from yesterday or today or even this very moment. What am I?

57. I Go Around and Around

I go around all the places in a city, town, and village, but I never can come inside. You will notice if I am not there, but if I am there, you hardly notice me. What am I, please?

58. Flying Without Wings

Wingless, I can fly fast or slow. When floating, I can be different colors. Eyeless, I can shed tears. What am I?

59. No Senses, But I Can Sense

I can experience the senses of sight, hearing, smelling, and taste with no tongue, notes, ears, or eyes. Some people may eat me, but you would not want to be around them. What am I?

60. Wrong Word

Simply put, pronouncing me correctly, you will always be wrong. Saying my name the right way, you are correct. Tell me what I am but try not to be wrong.

61. Locks and Unlocks

Even though I consist of keys, I have no locks. I may have space, but I have no room. Enter me, and you may escape, but you can't go outside. Can you guess what I am?

62. You Take Me

I am transported from a mine and encapsulated in a wooden case. While I cannot escape, being used worldwide is my thing. What am I?

63. Backwards Cheese

I am a cheese made in the reverse. Please tell me what I am.

64. Lots of Letters

I am a building that ends in the letter 'e' and starts with the letter 'p.' I may be small or large, but either size, I store thousands of letters, too. What am I?

65. A Type of Ship

I am a ship that has two mates but no captains in sight. What am I?

66. A Mini Tree

Even though I am a tree, you can fit me in your hand. Are you smart enough to tell me what I am?

67. Super Delicate

I am something that is very fragile and delicate. You have to listen to avoid breaking me. Speak my name and I am of no use. Tell me what I am.

68. One Head, not Human

I have one head, but I am not human. I have one foot and four legs. I may sound like a freak, but people are hardly scared of me. What am I?

69. Everyone Needs Me

Everyone in the world needs me. If more people used me, the world would be a better place. People always give me, but people hardly ever take me. I am cheaper than going to a therapist. What am I?

70. What Word

I am a word. When you add two letters to me, I get shorter. If you don't pay attention, I'm gone. May you tell me what I am?

71. A Vehicle

Now you see me. Briefly. Now you don't. Too bad. A type of vehicle, I am spelled the exact same way forwards and backwards. What am I?

72. What State

I am small yet popular. If you come here, you will never forget. I am a state that is surrounded by a lot of water and a place to come if you are ever upset. What am I?

73. Every Night

I come out every night without having to be called. I can twinkle or be dim. However, I can disappear just like I appear. I am lost every day without being stolen. What am I?

74. Center of Gravity

Don't overlook me, but you can if you're are not looking too closely. I am at the center of gravity. Without me, there is no such thing as gravity. Tell me what I am if you dare.

75. A Fruit

I am a fruit. If you take away my first letter, you will get a body part. If you take away the initial and last letter, a video game company I am. Do you know what I am?

76. No Flaky Hair

With ear, I am deaf. Having flakes, I am hairless. Can you take the challenge? Please explain what I am.

77. Pilgrim Music

I was the type of music that the early Pilgrims loved to listen to. What am I?

78. Dangerous

I can hurt you without moving an inch. I can poison you without touching you. I can tell the truth, and I can also lie. Size isn't a factor. Please say what I am.

79. A Man's Weakness

I weaken all men for hours each day. I show you weird visions while you are away. I take you by night, by day, I take you back. None suffer from having a lot of me, but they suffer from not having enough of me. What am I?

80. I Belong to You

I technically may be yours, but others may feel more inclined to it. Are you capable of telling me what I am?

81. I Can Be

Short. Long. Grown or used because I'm your own. Painted or blank. Square, coffin or stiletto. What I am depends on your guess.

82. I Have Just One

One for sure. Eight others to spare. Typically, I'm nice, but other times I'm ambivalent. Please guess what I am.

83. Men Hear Me

At the sound of me, loud or soft, men dream and move their feet. My sound, loud and or soft, causes men to cry or giggle. Will you be able to tell me what I am?

84. No Hinges

No hinges, screws, keys, or lock, yet a precious treasure is inside. Tell me what I am.

85. A Single Color

A single color but a multitude of colors. I may be at the bottom, but I can fly. You see me in the sun, and I disappear in the rain. Harmless and painless, can you tell me what I am?

86. Reach for the Sky

I may be gone if you don't pay attention, but I'm in the background. I strive for the sky, but I'm still around. What am I?

87. Three Letters

With just three letters, I am the same going the front way and going the back way. Tell me what word I am.

88. Sometimes white, sometimes black,

sometimes I am the brightest of whites, but most of the time, I am the darkest of blacks. I will take you there, but you will never come back. Traffic stops because of me, and I am often an overlooked part in people's history. What am I?

89. Green, red, or other

Sometimes red, sometimes green, and sometimes our color is in between. Some spray us. I can be hot or cold, but don't touch your eyes after touching me. What am I?

90. Many Legs

I may have lots of legs, but I am unable to stand. A long neck I have, but no head. Unable to walk and unable to see, I still keep things tidy. Tell me what I am, please.

91. An Insect

While I'm an insect, there is another insect within the first part of my name. A famous group even has a name like mine. Don't squash me when you see me. Please tell me what I am.

92. Many Feathers

Feathers help me soar, but it's up to you to tell me the distance I can go. I, not alive, but I have a head. Can you guess what I am?

93. The Tool of a Potato

The potato loves to use me because I am powerful. I can be used every 60 or 30 minutes. If my cells are gone, I am no longer a working tool. Tell me what I am if you dare.

94. No Lungs

I don't have any legs to tango, waltz, or do the polka. I am even lungless. I can dance and breathe even though I am not alive. Are you able to decipher what I am?

95. First in the Ocean

My initial letter is in the opera, but never in sync. My second letter is in waffle, but never in beetle. My third letter is in gloat and also in fly, which is exactly what I do at night. I'm begging you. Please tell me what I am.

96. Very Skinny

Slim and introverted, I only live for about 60 minutes, and then I'm gone. In the hour I'm alive, I eat all I can. When people see me, they are not happy, but when I leave, they hate it. Are you able to guess what I am?

97. Invisible, Yet There

Unable to be touched, seen, or felt, I am in every single being. Some people argue if I am alive or not, but there is a genre of music that is my namesake. Please tell me what I am if you are smart enough.

98. Skinny and Lean

I am lean and skinny and many like that. You experience good feelings when you touch me, albeit, short-lived. I only shine once and then no more after that. Can you tell me what I am?

99. To Measure or to Not Measure

You won't know me until you measure me, but when I am flown, you will miss me because I'm gone. Are you smart? Are you capable? Can you figure me out? What am I?

100. White and Grind

White is my color. Cutting and grinding are my things, but if I am broken, you have to fill or remove me. I can be sharp or dull or real or fake. Whatever it is, you'll want me when you're eating steak. What am I?

101. Walk on Four Legs

Four. Two. Three. This explains how many legs I walk on at the beginning, middle, and end of my life respectively. What am I?

102. Cannot Control Me

Humans make me, but they have no power on me. I suck on different things like flesh or paper and sometimes all at the same time. I can be more harmful than helpful at times. I am a tornado of energy and can be everywhere all the time. Tell me what I am if you can.

103. Try and Catch Me

I am everywhere, but not seen. I am captured, but not helped. I have no throat to speak, but you will hear me. Are you able to figure out what I am about? Can you tell me what I am?

104. One Blind Eye

I only have one eye, but it is not used to see. I may enjoy the ocean, but I am unable to have fun and swim in it. I am white on my back and gray on my stomach. I may come, but I don't stay too long. Can you tell me what I am, please?

105. Different Colors

When you first get me, I am black. When you put me to use, I turn red. And I transform into white when you're all done with me. Some people love me, but if you use me without asking it could end in disaster. What am I?

106. Pointed Teeth

My pointy teeth wait for my next victim. When I got you, you will know, you'll feel my bite from head to toe. My victims normally don't have any blood, but you sure wouldn't want me to bite you. Are you able to figure out what I am?

107. No Eyes

I don't have an eye now, but I used to be able to see. I once had thoughts, but I am now empty. I used to be full of vim, but not I am lean and trim. What am I?

108. Weight in My Belly

I can be heavy because I have a solid stomach, and my back is made of trees. Nails pierce my ribs, but I don't have any feet. Doesn't matter how much weight I carry, I'll get it done, whether fast or slow. What am I?

109. Cannot Be Seen

You can't see me. You can't hear me. You can't smell me. I reside behind the balls in the sky and hide before hills. I always fill in the holes that are empty. I exist first and then after that. I stop life and the joy of laughter. I am tricky, I know. Can you tell me what I am?

110. Light and Hidden

I am made of something but lighter than that. Most of me is hidden, but you'll still want to be careful. Care to tell me what I am?

111. Between Your Head and Toes

Toes and head are what you use me in between. The more you use me, the smaller I get. What am I?

112. Different Sizes and Shapes

Straight or curves, patterns and shapes are many that I come in. I go wherever you want, but there is only one way I truly go. Are you able to tell me the thing that I am?

113. Sleep Throughout the Day

Unlike you, I sleep in the day, and I fly in the darker day without having any feathers. Tell me what I am if you can.

114. Travel Low and High

I go low and I go high. You can find me between any line if you read them. If there is no me, there is no sound in the world. Please tell me what I am.

115. None Seeps

Liquid can get on me, but I will not get wet. If you hit me, I am like a chameleon and can change colors. I cover lots of things, I'm quite complex. Can you tell me what I am?

116. Thirty Men

Thirty men and two ladies are what I consist of. We just stand around. Still, we look great. However, if we move about, a fight will break out. Are you able to tell me what I am?

117. Often Held

You can hold me without touching me. I can't rust even though I am perpetually wet. I can bite but more rarely bitten. Some have me but can't use me. I may be guessed if you are smart.

118. Up and Down

I can go down and up simultaneously. I am both the present and the past tense. Are you ready to go for a ride? What word I am is up to you.

119. Tear Me Off

You can rip me and put scratches on my noggin. I'm black now even though I used to be red. Careful, careful, try not to singe a finger or you will have one painful member. What am I?

120. Fingers—Nope

I don't have any fingers, but I have two arms. I cannot run, but I have two feet. I can carry things the best when my feet are off the ground. Please tell me what I am if you can.

121. Crack a Smile

I prefer smiles over frowns. But whatever you give me, I'll adjust automatically. When you drop me, I often crack. However, if you give me a lovely smile, right back at you, I'll give the smile back. Are you able to tell me what thing I am?

122. Always Old

I am always old, but sometimes I am new. I can be blue but never sad. I am sometimes full but never empty. I do not push, but I always pull. What am I?

123. Loud Noise

Watch out. Switching out my jacket will cause a huge sound. I weigh less even though I look larger. Are you able to tell me what I am?

124. You Hear

You heard me before, and you'll hear me again. Then I will die until you call me again. What am I?

125. What Letter

Rock I am, but I am not stone. In marrow, you can find me but not in bone. Find me in the bolster, but you will not find me in bed. Nowhere in living, and I am not in the dead. What am I?

126. Ruler of Shovels

There may not be many people who want to be a ruler of shovels, but I do, and I love my job. For some people, I am the end goal. I am one of a double and thin like a knife blade. Oh yeah, I have a wife. Tell me what I am.

127. Fingers Equal Four

No blood and no flesh, but I have a thumb and fingers that equal four. Are you able to tell me what the thing is that I am?

128. The Pope Does Not Use It

He does not use it, but the Pope has it. Your mom uses it just like your dad. The husband of your girlfriend has it, and she also uses it. Do you know what I am?

129. Invisible Roots

The roots I have are invisible. The trees are not as tall as me, but I do not grow. You're a genius if you can tell me what I am.

130. Nothing on the Outside

On the inside and on the outside, there is nothing. Twenty men can't lift me, although I am lighter than paper. What am I?

131. Beauty in the Sky

Beautiful and magical all throughout the sky, I just can't fly. I'm good luck to some, and others think I bring them riches. Please tell me what I am.

132. No Drinks from This

No one can drink me, and I am a fountain. For people who search me, I am like gold. However, the more I continually die, I bring riches to everyone who wants more. Tell me what I am if you can, please.

133. A Precious Stone

Clear like a diamond, I am considered a precious stone. Find me when the sun is close to the horizon. My power helps you walk on water, but if you keep me, I will be gone in an hour. Are you able to tell me what I am?

134. A Beamer

Beaming, shining, sparkling white, the day becomes brighter when I am around from a single light. Enchanting and charming, that's what I do to all. Bringing out the best in you is what I do to you all. Can you please tell me what I am?

135. I Devour

Flowers, beasts, birds, and trees are all the things that I devour. Really, I devour everything. I eat iron and steel easily and make hard stones dust. I kill famous men and cause mountains to go down, plus I ruin towns. What am I?

136. I Am Small

Tiny, but bigger than a bee, I am nimble like a flea, except I don't buzz. I hum my songs. I love delectable flower nectar. What am I?

137. I Am Big

Huge and bulky, my long trunk is like a tree. I keep water in my nose which is like a hose. What am I?

138. I March Before Armies

I am ahead of armies and people love to give me their attention. If I fall, it's over but not because I've been killed. I love the wind, and the wind loves my non-legged self. What am I if you can guess?

139. Beginning of Ideas

You don't think of me, but I am an important part of history. I am at the beginning of lots of good ideas. But if you don't like your idea, crumble and toss me out. Tell me what I am.

140. My Children

Near and far is where my children are, but I can always find them. I give them gifts to make them happy, but if I leave, my children are going away. Can you tell me what I am?

141. I Can Fall

If I fall off a skyscraper, I will be okay, but if I fall into the water, it's a quick, slow death. What am I?

142. Can You See

If you pause and observe, you can see me. If you try to feel me, you are not able to. If you come close to me, I will move from you even though I can't move. Are you able to tell me what I am?

143. You Have Me

You have me today. Tomorrow, you'll have more. As your time passes, I'm not easy to store. I don't take up space, but I am only in one place. I am what you saw but now what you see. What am I?

144. In You

I am always in you and sometimes on you. If I surround you, I can kill you. I hope you can figure me out.

145. Cracked

Cracked, told, played, and made are all things that I can do. Please guess what I am.

146. I Am Red

I am red, blood pumps through me, and I live throughout your physical body. Love is what I realize. Can you tell me what I am if you don't mind?

147. Sweet Rest

You can use me when you're resting. I am soft and comfortable, and I protect your neck and head. You can ask for me on an airplane, and fighting with me can be fun. What am I?

148. Soup or Burger

You can find me in soup or on a hamburger. When raw, I am green, but when ripened, I am red and becomes a savory condiment. What am I?

149. Children Love Me

Children love to play with me, but not inside, only out. Watch out for the wires and trees for you could tangle me. Look up and watch me dance. The faster you run, the faster I will wiggle. What am I?

150. The Ocean Is My Home

The ocean is my real home. It is common you find me in red, pink, blue, or gold. Humans trick me into biting. My favorite thing is blowing bubbles, and if you take me home with you, I will be an easy pet to take care of. What am I?

151. Don't Drop Me

I can connect you to the world even though sometimes you ignore me. I am covered with buttons, and my sounds can be unique. Don't drop me, or I might crack. What am I?

152. I Wiggle

I can't see, but I wiggle. On a tree, you can find me, which I prefer over being on a hook. Even if you don't realize it, sometimes I am in a book. Are you able to tell me what I am if you are good enough to figure it out?

153. The Special Room

You can't come in, even though I am a room. Sometimes I am poisonous, and sometimes I am delicious to eat.
What am I?

154. Wave Me

Waving my hands is a symbol of leaving even though I cannot actually say good-bye. Use me when you're hot, and I will cool you off. What am I?

155. Three Eyes

One leg. Three eyes. Listen to me, or you might get into trouble. What am I?

156. Forward and Backward

Forward and backwards, I go every day. Different sizes, colors, and shapes are what I come in. Some I might fright, but for most, they go night-night. What am I?

157. Long Tail

My tail is long. My coat can be black or grey. I live in the house of which I live outside. I come out to have fun when you are in dreamland. Please tell me what I am.

158. Carry Me

Carry me with you, and I will keep your hair dry. Short or long I can be, opened or closed. I'm not a problem unless you use me in the house. What am I?

159. No Voice

I teach you with no voice. No spines or hinges I have, not even a door. I tell you what you need to know, then I go. Are you able to tell me what I am?

160. Different Colors

Many beautiful different colors are what I come in. I smell nice, and you can pick me up if you want. I will live for a long time as long as you water me. Guess what you can to tell me what I am.

161. Bigger When Full

There are many different colors that I come in. I will float away if you don't tie me down, and I will make a loud sound if I break. What am I?

162. Brick Body

My body is usually made of brick or wood, and I come with a lot of windows and doors. Keep me clean for visitors, and I will keep you warm and cozy. You can sell me if your family grows. What am I?

163. Keep Me Away

I am the enemy of paper, and small children shouldn't be around me. Create me when you're doing art or when you're doing your hair. Tell me what I am.

164. Easily Overlooked

No one pays attention to me even though we all have one. If you can, are you able to tell me what I am?

165. The Harder You Run

You can run very hard, but it will be more difficult for you to capture me. Please tell me what I am.

166. Twirl My Body

Twirling my body is what I do, but I keep my head very high. Once I'm in, it's very difficult to remove me. Guess what I am.

167. A Seed

I have three letters in my name and with all three, I am a type of see. When you take away the last two letters, I still sound the same. Try and figure me out.

168. Going Up

Up and up I go, and I don't come down. As I go higher, my wrinkle count goes up too. Can you please tell me what I am?

169. Green Jacket

I am a green, white, and red sandwich with lots of black sprinkled throughout. Are you able to figure me out?

170. Black as Night

I'm very dark, and I have three eyes. I can knock down 10 in one go. Please tell me if you are able to guess me.

171. Good at Hiding

I help you be courageous, but I hide the truth. If you can figure me out, you're great.

172. Pure, But Forgotten

I can be rotten every now and then, but I am always around you although you forget. Tell me what I am.

173. Run

You combine my bodies together, and when I am not moving, I run. Are you able to tell me what thing I am?

174. A Mother

My kids are equal to the number eight, and I turn all day even though I have weight. There was a ninth kid before I realized it was fake. Can you tell me what I am?

175. Never Stolen

I am unable to be taken from because I am collectively owned, although some people have less, and some have more. Can you please guess what I am?

176. Enjoyed by Some

   I will be here forever unless you get rid of me. Some people
   love me, and others hate me, but I'm not that bad if you do it
   right. What am I?

177. Soft and Hairy

   Sort, hairy, and I stretch from door to door. I'm always on
   the floor. Tell me what I am. I know you can.

178. A Ring

   No fingers, but a ring I have. Typically, I am still, but now I
   can follow you wherever you go. Tell me what I am.

179. Take Off My Clothes

   Your clothes go, mine come on. My clothes come on, your
   clothes go. I know you can do it. Please tell me what I am.

180. Metal or Bone

   You may want me to bite you because my bite does not hurt.
   Wood, metal, or bone are my ingredients. Are you able to
   figure out what this is about?

181. Run Around

Back and forth, I go throughout the day, but I rest when I'm done. I'm so tired that my tongue is out at the end of the day. Can you tell me what I am?

182. The Protector

I protect people. That's what I do. Sitting on a bridge is what I do even though people can see straight through me. Some people want to know what's underneath. Can you figure me out?

183. An Absolute Necessity

Some people need me, and they love me when among family and friends. I can be hot or cold but enjoyable for all, doesn't matter if it's light or dark. When you finish drinking me, I leave my mark. Are you able to tell me what I am?

184. Not Born

I am here even though I am not birthed. I have lots of names, but I am not given an official name and birthed by life and science. Figure me out if you can.

185. In the Rainforest

Everywhere you go, you may not find me. But if you are in a rainforest, you will see me with my weird number of toes. I'm probably chilling upside down and very lazy. See if you can figure me out.

186. Buttons or a Zipper

I have buttons or a zipper, pockets or sometimes a belt. I'll protect you from a cold wind, but you won't need me in the summer. When you are done with me, please hang me in the closest. What am I?

187. Jump and Climb

I can jump, and I can climb. With my many legs, I swing from tree to tree. I can make a house much bigger than me. What am I?

188. Go Up

I am round. Up and down, I go. Catching and throwing me is what you can do, but use caution near windows. Figure me out.

189. Keep You Entertained

I will keep you entertained with my drama and my comedy. I am shaped like a cube, and I can attach to your wall. What am I?

190. Curly and Bald

You can call me curly, and you can call me bald. You can call me gray, you can call me shaggy. Long or short is what I can be. Tell me what I am, please.

191. In the Woods

In the woods is where you got me. When you sat down is when you found me. And it hurts, but it's okay. Please tell me what I am.

192. Wake You

I can wake you in the morning without electricity, batteries, or winding. What am I?

193. Lick, Lick

I am a delicious treat that you can lick with your tongue. I come in a cone or in a bowl. One of my common flavors is also a common scent. What am I?

194. Fruit

Good taste and lots of energy are what I give when you eat me. I may be your favorite fruit. Single people can like me. You can also find me in a calendar in lots of boxes. What am I?

195. Two Meanings

Two meanings are what I hold. One is broken, and the other holds on. Are you able to tell me what I am?

196. A Food

Five letters are what I have. When you take away the first letter, I give you energy. Take away the first two letters, and I am necessary to life. Take away the last three letters, and you can drink me. Have at it. Figure out what I am.

197. I Am Scary

I exit your ears and cause fear in others. I am quiet, like mice, but no one wants me in their house. Can you tell me what I am?

198. A Small Piece of Paper

Small yet valuable, I am only a piece of paper. You need me for big events and travel. Tell me what I am.

199. Can Be Embarrassing

Sometimes people get embarrassed when you stand on me and a whole lot of people watch. Women hate me and stand on me in secret. Can you tell me what I am?

200. People Walk in Me

Come and go inside of me. You push me, and I will do what you say. When you leave me, I wait for the next command and the next person to come into my life. Can you please tell me what I am?

Chapter 2: Super Hard Riddles — "What Am I?"

1. At the Beginning

At the beginning of end, at the end of place. At the end of space and time, and at the beginning of place. Can you figure out what I am?

2. First in Bridge

In bridge, but not ridge is my first letter. In awake, but not in mistake is my second letter. The third is not in ranger but in danger. The fourth letter is in gooey, but not in ooey. My fifth is in spine, and the last is in winter. Tell me what I am.

3. Creature of Power

I am a creature of power and a creature of grace, a creature of beauty and a creature of strength. I set everything in the world's pace, for all things in the world must stay under my green influence. Can you please let me know what I am?

4. Sisters That Are Two

We are sisters that are two. One is bright, and one is dark. We stay in twin homes, and people love us together. Who are we?

5. Four-Letter Word

I am a versatile word consisting of four letters. No matter how you read me, I am the same. Can you tell me what you think I am?

6. The Traveling Letter

I can move from over here to over there by going way and then come here to there by coming back again. What letter will you say that I am?

7. Covered in White

I cover the rolling hills in white. While I am not able to swallow, I can definitely bite. What am I?

8. White and Dirty

I am something that most people have come in contact with. I am difficult to clean because the whiter I am, the dirtier I get. What am I?

9. Hard Tongue

My tongue isn't soft, so you can really hear me speak. Since I'm lungless, I can't breathe. I can be loud or soft even though I don't have a voice. What am I?

10. Letters Equal to Six

This word means a group but erasing the first letter means wood that burns. Tell me what I am.

11. Three Lives

Three lives I have. Crack rocks, sooth skin, and hugging the sky are all things that I do. Can you please tell me what I am?

12. Sky and Ground

Ground and in the sky are where you can find me. I always end with an f. What am I?

13. Fall and Break

I fall, but I am unbreakable. Even if I break, I don't fall in order to do so. I am what two things?

14. Water of Life

I am the water of life but seeing too much of me is never good. I am what brings families together, but I can be defied. What am I?

15. Forward

When you see me forward, I weigh a ton. But when you see me backwards, I do not. Please tell me what I am.

16. Feel Me, But Can't See

    Touch me, but you can't use your eyes to see me. You shiver
    when I come and are relieved when I pass. What am I?

17. With Me

    Although I don't get wet, I am used in a bath. Tell me what I
    am if you can?

18. Red Tears

    My tears are red when you squeeze, but I have a heart made
    of stone. What am I?

19. Use Me Everyday

    You use me every day but let me rest at night. I have an exact
    twin with me all the time. And somehow, you always cover
    me up. I have a soul but not alive. What am I?

20. Creative Memories

    You can hear me and feel me, but you can't see me or smell
    me, yet everyone has a taste in me. I can be created, but after
    that only remembered. What am I?

21. Served

Served in two or four, tiny, circular and white, I am fun when you see me at a table. Please let me know what I am.

22. Out from Earth

They sell me in the mart, and I come out from earth. When you purchase me, off my tail goes and my silk suit. But you cry when I am dead. Are you able to guess what I am?

23. Dog's Name

I am a dog's name consisting of only one letter and one number. What am I?

24. Straight Through Me

I move like lighting, so fast that you can't watch me. Everyone can see right through me, and I go forever, even until the day you die. Can you please let me know what I am?

25. Negative Magic

Magic I am, but reality I show. However, making your hand on the right, transform to your left, and your hand on the left transform into your right. Tell me what I am.

26. Share but Selfish

You can share me, but still have me all to yourself. What am I?

27. I Am Two

There is one in room, and in the corner, there are two, but shelter only has one. Can you tell me what I am?

28. Thunder Before Lightning

Thunder arrives in the moments before the lightning. The lightning comes in the moments before the rain, and rain makes all the ground dry that it touches. Are you capable of figuring me out?

29. Five and Six

Once you put six and five together, you get eleven, but when you take the numbers seven and six together, you get the number one. Can you guess what I am?

30. Give Me Away

People need me, some more than others, but they always give me away. You give me intentionally away for a gift or unintentionally for carelessness. What am I?

31. Starts with Gas

I start with gas and have 10 letters. What am I?

32. Run Around

I run all around the pasture, but I never move. I can be around your house, too. What am I?

33. Shave Beards

I shave beards all day, but I still have a beard. Who am I?

34. Which Word

This entire word means an awesome woman, but the first two letters mean a man, and the first three letters mean a woman, and the first four mean an awesome man. Which word am I?

35. Past Is the Past

The past is where I stay. The present is where I'm made, but the future can't touch me. Are you able to guess what I am correctly?

36. See Me in Water

The water is where you will find me, all dry of course. What am I?

37. My Brother

You see my brother, not me. You can hear me, but not him. Where I am, my brother is, too. What am I and who is my brother?

38. I Travel Alone

I travel alone, never lonely. My name is real, but I don't exist. What am I?

39. Summertime Favorite

Friends like to have me. I am not living, but I still grow. Oh yeah, I'm a summertime favorite. Can you figure me out?

40. Sweet or Sour

I'm not a rhyming word but have sweetness and some sour. Are you able to tell me what I am?

41. Compliments People

The digit that compliments people is my first. The second digit points to things. The digit to hurt people is my third one. The fourth digit may just hold a treasure, and fancy people love my fifth digit when they drink things. Are you capable of figuring out what I am?

42. A Circle

I'm essentially a circle, nothing really, but I'm worth tenfold. Are you able to tell me what I am?

43. Two in a Whole

I am two in a whole and four in a pair. Six in a trio you see. Eight's a quartet but what you must get is the name that fits just one of me. What am I?

44. Digging a Tiny Cave

Dig and dig is what I do, putting silver and gold where holes used to be. Tell me what I am if you can?

45. Simple or Complex

Shapes. Colors. Complex. Simple. I am all of that and found in daily life. Perhaps even in this riddle. Can you figure out what I am?

46. Some People

Count, consume, avoid are all things that people do to me. Can you tell me what I am?

47. It May Sound

It may sound as if I work in the transport industry, but I really work in fine dining. Do you know what I am?

48. Shimmery Field

I am a far-reaching shimmery swatch of land without noticeable tracks but crossable. What am I?

49. Write on Me

I keep secrets. You can write on me even though like a top I am because I spin. I can be used as a mop even though I can be used as a board, as well. You got it. See if you can let me know what I am.

50. Folding

Folding paper is how you can get me even if you do your best to avoid me. I'm small but painful. May you guess me?

51. Two Occupants

We live together two at a time, but sometimes you can squeeze in three. You eat my insides and throw my outsides away. What am I?

52. Walking and Running

When you walk, you know it's running. When I run, you know I'm walking. Are you able to figure out what I am?

53. Not My Name

My name is not my own and no one cares about me when they are on top. People shed tears when they see me and stay by my side night plus day. Tell me what I am if you can.

54. In Window

I'm white and very popular to have at a very popular event among people. Peaceful, I'm still a bird, bringing good news since the days of Noah. Will you tell me what I am?

55. You Can't Hide

You don't know when I am coming, but I am coming. Some expect me, and others don't. Just try to be ready when I arrive. Do you know what I am?

56. Brown Is What I Am

I smell like something purses are made of and you can put me on horses or on men. Tell me what I am, and you win this riddle.

57. The Path

You can use me as a path between things made by nature and as a path by things made by men. Can you tell me what I am?

58. Once a God

I used to be called a god, and for some people, I am still their angel. You either hate me or love me. Are you able to figure out what I am?

59. Soft Like Silk

I am soft like a pillow, white a cloud, and puffy like a tutu. I am the nastiest part of the tool you use to clean the floor. Please figure me out if you can.

60. Two-Faced

Two-faced and many people have fought over me. I may be small, but you wished that you had me every time you go through a toll or need to use a parking meter. Tell me what I am if you can.

61. Very Tempting

My coat can be smooth or pock-marked, yellow, green, or red. My insides are sweet and can be sweet or sour. You should love to pick me because I can save you a trip to the doctor. In some circles, I'm considered a temptation. Can you figure me out?

62. Young and Great

I am more valuable when I am older than when I am younger. Stepping on me may seem crazy, but it's the best thing to do. If you keep me long enough, you may have a small inheritance. Are you smart enough to figure out what I am?

63. My Title

I have pages, but I'm not a book. I have a title, but I'm not a book. I am a killer and slave, but I'm still not a book. Try to tell me what I am if you can.

64. Head Bob

I'm a head bobber with white hair and a cutesy yellow face. By the way, most of my body is green. Can you guess what I am?

65. Head or Tail

Head or tail, I'm perfect either way. Can you tell me what I am?

66. Add the Letter 'S'

Most people add the letter 's' to a word to make it mean more than one. But I'm special. I am a word that becomes plural when you add the letter 'C' instead. What am I?

67. More Shoes

Most of the shoes I have equal more than what anybody else can have. However, I have no feet. In the morning, you see me, but at night, I'm gone. I will shake when I am angry, but I am not going to bite. Are you able to tell me what I am?

68. Your Mechanic's Name

I am a mechanic's name. When your physical life is over, I may just have all your wealth. Can you get it? Can you figure out? Can you tell me what I am?

69. Beneath Your Roof

I live with you while you are alive, and I can live with you while you die. You need me to pay taxes, and you need me to write. Please guess what I am.

70. Evil Cutter

I fight for right, and I cut through evil just like butter. Not too far to the right and not too far to the left, I am all about being fair. Guess me if you can.

71. I Have Two

Two things I have, so you can have one, and I can have one. If you ask me about the price, I just nod my head and give you a smile. What can I be?

72. Want a Sweet

When craving sweetness, I am the place that you should come. If you can't stand the heat, then you need to get out. Are you able to tell me what I am?

73. Busy, Busy

On many busy streets, you will find me. If you keep me fed, you will be happy. But if you make me hungry, you're going to hate me. Please tell me what I am.

74. I Heard of a Wonder

I am an interesting person, half animal, half-human, all intelligence. You will see me in a coffee shop or library near you. But you may overlook me if you didn't have this clue. Can you tell me what I am?

75. Moving Slow

I am extremely slow moving, but if you want me to go faster, you can find assistance in the store. I am everywhere on some people and on others I'm sparer, but if you have none, you'll wish I was there. Explain what I am if you dare.

76. Take a Spin

Take me for a spin, and I'll make you cool, but use me in the winter, and you're a big fool. What am I?

77. Bury Me

Interestingly, when I am alive, you put me in the ground, but you dig me up when there is no more life in my body. Can you figure me out?

78. I Can Help You See

Castle-builder, mountain-destroyer, man-blinder, but sometimes I can help men see. Guess what I am.

79. Born of Water

I am born of water, and I drown in water. I am a blood-thirsty beast that you can barely see. What am I?

80. You Will Face Me

Face me and be happy. Most young people love me, although, older people tend to dislike me. Even if you forget me, that will not stop me from happening. Tell me what I am, please, if you can.

81. Silver-tongued

I am teary-eyed but never once dropped a tear. I am silver-tongued but never lived. I am double-winged but never fly, and I am air-cooled but never dry. What am I?

82. Twelve Is Left

I have six total letters, but when you just take one of those letters away, twelve is actually left. Can you make this math makes sense? Please tell me what I am.

83. White Father, Black Child

I am black, but my dad is white. I don't have any wings, but I fly to the heavens. When you meet me, you may cry, even though there is no reason to cry. However, at my birth, I go back into thin air. Are you able to tell me what I am?

84. Alive Without a Breath

Chilly like death, alive without having to breathe, I always drink, so my thirst is always quenched. Figure me out if you can.

85. Visible to You

If I am there, you are not able to see me. When I am away, you will wish to be assured of my presence. If you are slow and thoughtful, I am in abundance. But if you are fast and rash, I am hardly around. Are you able to tell me what I am?

86. Speak the Truth

I speak to you without talking. Everything in it is a lie, but that doesn't stop you from believing it. I am the source of countless joy of many across the world. Just suspend your disbelief. What am I?

87. Creatures of the Air

We are creatures of speech, yet everyone needs us no matter what language you speak. We are only five, but we are powerful. Without us, there would be a whole lot less words. Think really hard but not too deep. Soon enough, you'll find the answer that you seek.

88. Peep, Peep

My sister is young, and she does a double peep. She goes throughout the waters very deep. She climbs as high as she can on the mountains, but unfortunately, she only has one eye socket. Who can I be?

89. Utensil Love

Bread or a paper cutter is what I am being used for. Thugs or wives use me, one for nefarious means and the other for means not so nefarious. What am I?

90. A Hundred Years

I have been here for over one hundred years. I give food and find food on my own consisting of rain and sun to name a few. I don't move much, but when I do, you will be able to use me for other things. If you think long and hard, you can figure me out. What do you think I am?

91. Helping Engines

Pants or engines, I help both of them function. Think, and you can figure me out.

92. They Belong to Me

I am mine, and I am yours. I can make you feel all types of emotions from yellow to blue. I will keep going until the day that you do not go any more. Figure me out, and tell me what I am.

93. Round Am I

Similar to a round chess-board, I can be curled and whirled. Some play me personally or watch me from their home, but anyone can play me if they want to bad enough. What am I?

94. Beautiful and Cold

Cold and beautiful, old, and young, alive, and always dead. When you feed me, I'm still hungry. I can die if I bleed enough or if you chop my head off. Can you figure out what I am?

95. Lovely and Round

I am round and lovely, shining with a pale light, brought up in the dark, the joy of many women. Please tell me what I am if you can.

96. End of My Yard

Twenty-four women are dancing in my year in green gowns and blue hats. Tell me what I am if you can.

97. Makes No Sense

I make absolutely no sense. If you are in me, you will either fall hard or fly high. I make you do everything because my need is a necessity of biology but an illogical anomaly. I'm not real, but if you work hard, you can achieve them if you believe in yourself. What am I?

98. First a Blessing

I was a blessing sent to earth after the flowers and plants were nourished. Then I was sent as a reminder for hope, and I'm not too bad on the eyes. If you guess me, I will be surprised. Can you tell me what I am?

99. Used for Light

While solid, I am used for light. If I am not around, you will feel trapped. I do not like to be touched. Oh yeah, I enjoy being in buildings. Say ye, what I am?

100. Backbite

I rarely walk even though I have lefts. I will never speak, but I will backbite. I look for places that can hide me. What am I you say? You tell me.

101. I Can Wave

I will wave at you, but it's not to say goodbye. When I am up high, you are especially cool with me. Can you figure out what I am?

102. Forest Without Trees

Similar to a forest without trees is what I am. Similar to a jail you want to visit because the inmates are innocent. Don't feed the inmates, and you can walk wherever you want to. What am I?

103. Heavy Feet

People have heavy feet when they come to visit me. I hold one, and when I am able to, I will dance, turn, and spin. What do you think I am? What can I possibly be?

104. Day Sleeping

I hide and sleep through the day because I am up all night. I shine briefly in comparison to when I sleep. Watch out or you will miss me. Can you guess the right answer to what I am?

105. Lacking Reason

I rhyme but don't make much sense. That's why you need logic as one of my requirements. The words you need for your kinfolk or your friends are there if you look within. By the way, the answer is basically in my name. Can you tell me what I am?

106. I Drink

I am more poisonous than the venom found in snakes. Quietly, I drink in fluids that are darker than the night. I beat the mightiest of warriors but not in a fight. Can you figure out what I am?

107. A Tradition

Once upon a long time ago, I used to be a very important tradition during the dark ages. Men did magical things like transforming the dark into the light and by mixing magic potions, supposedly in the night. Unfortunately, the efforts didn't work because they were burned as witches. What tradition would you say that I am?

108. Small and Light

Even though I am small, I am full of light. Don't forget me because you need me to shine in the night. I can help light up whatever pyre you want because I am able to start fires. What am I?

109. Four Total Legs

I don't have an ounce of hair, but I have a total of four whole legs. I am always ready to work even though people ride me for hours. I don't go anywhere without you giving me a nudge. What would you say that I am?

110. Daily Dawn

Daybreak and dawn could not happen without me at all. Daisies also grow from me, and the sun sometimes isn't found. But forget the sun, I am around. What can I be?

111. Only the Maker

When you buy me, I am worth nothing. Only the person who makes me know how much it truly costs. Rich kings or the poorest of men give me easily. If I am a broker, deceit and pain can be the results. What will you guess that I am?

112. A Delectable Thing

A most delectable thing, you give me away because you cannot keep me. After you sleep, you may awaken to me as I am soft and moist like a dragonfly wing, but watch out, I can sting. What am I?

113. In a Box

I am contained in a box full of very rare things. No flute. No hair. Would I be? I am very soft in the bed that I won but rock solid. Dim in the dark, I only shine if no longer locked. What would you guess that I am?

114. Moved and Rolled

Moved I can be. Rolled I can be. But you will be able to hold nothing. Blue, red, and other colors I can be even though I don't have a head. I am also eyeless, but I am all over the place. What would you say that I am?

115. Left or Right

Right and left are both ways that I can be used while traveling over bumpy gravel or cobblestone. When used upward, I try for success. When used downwards, I am stressed. What will you say that I am?

116. A Staple Food

You can cook me a lot of different ways, and I come in a lot of different flavors. I'm found in pantries all over the world. Sometimes, it only takes one minute. What am I?

117. Wings Totaling Four

The number of wings I have is four, but I do not fly. My body is able to move around, but I like to stay in the same spot. I chew for a person before they are fed. What am I?

118. First in a Family

My first can be found in family, but not in sweet. The second is in rent, but not in pale. My third is in underwear, but not in town. My fourth is in tiny, but not in scepter. My fifth is in teeth if you look closely. My entire word means a delicious snack for us all. What will you say that I am?

119. Softly Tread

If you walk softly on me, I can take you a gajillion places. I can be very high or very low, and often quite flat in the middle. Kids love me, and adults tolerate me. Figure me out if you can.

120. I Am a Tool

Buy me in the store for a little under or a little over a penny. I am used to inspiring me. Don't overdo me or my effectiveness will no longer be there. Can you tell me what I am?

121. Shifting Around

I only move a small number of inches at a time, but when I move, I go extremely slow. If I move too much, I will be responsible for lots of deaths. Even though I am gigantic, I am not seen by people. Do you know what I am?

122. Women

A few women could care less about being described this way, even though it's a misconception that every woman wants this. It is a crybaby and very loud but transforms when you give it toys. Please tell me what I am.

123. Ancient Stones

I am a bunch of stones put together to protect lots of bones. You can add some riches in there too. I look like a very popular shape. Are you able to say what I am?

124. Glitters

Glitter — yes. Glitter — no. Hot or cold I can be. The eye cannot see my constant changes, but inside me are lots of important things. Some find safety behind me, and others may die under me. Broken I am, old, too, but I bring life forth. What am I if you can guess?

125. Don't Breathe

I jump high and run long even though I don't breathe. I can stretch and swim even though I don't eat. Standing and sleeping are what I do but I do not drink. I may not be able to think, but I can grow and play. Eyeless, I cannot see, but you can see me. Are you able to tell me what I am?

126. Known to Be Deceitful

I once was known as a deceiver despite being held in high esteem. No legs I have, but I can get around and tend to scare lots of people in the process. What am I?

127. More Than Life

Men love me more than life, but they fear me more than death. All men take me to the grave, but the poor have it, rich people don't need me, but if you're content, you're okay with me. Are you able to tell me what I am?

Nothing

128. Caught in My Trap

You can get caught in my trap because I trap many things of different colors and things. I'm never boring because I change a lot. Can you please tell me what I am?

light?

129. Wealthy

I tend to stand in water and flourish in wealth. I am valued over the land because I am a fencer. I am famous for farmers, but huntsmen despise me. You could possibly experience ruin if I am broken. Can you tell me what I am?

130. First Master

Four legs are how many my first master has. Two legs are how many my second master has. The first master is served in death, and the second master is served in death. I am soft but tough and love to rest on the cheeks of ladies. Are you able to tell me what I am?

131. Weird Creature

I am weird. Words to describe me include straight, metallic, tough, and super long. I puff and squeal and can help a lot of lives move to and from. Can you say what I am?

132. Bleed Without Blood

I do not beat even though I am a heart. No blood, but I can bleed if I am cut. Wingless, I can fly and finless, I can swim. Mouthless, I can sing. Guess what I am.

133. Tender Voice

Slender waist, tender voice, people invite me to play. Everywhere I go, I have to take a bow, or I will have nothing to say. Please tell me what I am if you can.

134. Slippery Fish

I will slip right through your fingers if you are not careful. A spear or a hook cannot catch me, but you'll need to use your hand to capture me. Can you tell me what I am?

135. Love of Mine

I love to see your chalky beauty in whatever formation you are in. If I pay attention, I can see your bright orbs amongst tiny lights. What would you say I am?

136. In My Entirety

In my entirety, I am very safe. If you take my head off, we can meet. If you take my head off, I will be ready. When you put my head back, I become a place for the beasts. Are you able to guess what I am?

137. Two Little Brothers

We are two little brothers. We help some win, and we help some lose. Roll us once, you may like us. Roll us again you may hate us. What can we be?

138. Soft and Cuddly

I am soft and cuddly. I'll put at your heartstrings, but take my last name by itself, and I'll tear you apart. What am I?

139. I Catch Warmth

Who catches heat and traps it? I do. Who brings water and ice to the earth? I do. What can slip through your fingers? I can. What am I?

140. Open Barrel

I look like a piece of honeycomb, but I'm full of soft flesh that is alive. What say you that I am?

141. Keep Things Green

In the summer, I keep many men happy and make children even happier. I bring a life force so strong that the grass loves when I come on. What am I?

142. Red Liquid

Although I am not a safe box, you put a life-saving red fluid inside of me. Please guess what I am.

143. Whoever Makes Me

If I make you, I'm not telling others. If you take me, you'll never know until it's too late. What am I?

144. Empty Inside

I am a useful thing, firm, hard, and white. I am empty inside and can work while being wet or dry. Doctors love me and parents with toddlers hate me. Are you able to guess what I am?

145. English Word

An English word I am. I have 3 sets of double letters in a row. What word am I?

146. Two eyes

Eyes in my front and eyes on my tail, but more eyes on my tail than in the front. Can you guess what I am?

147. Flora

Flora, foliage, and shrubbery are all things that describe me. Fauna, trees, grass are things that do not describe me. Can you tell me what I am?

148. Turn Me Over

Before you sell me, you may turn me over. If you travel far, you may turn me over as well. Can you figure me out?

149. Unique Teeth

I have unique teeth that can get the job done if the hardest force and show of strength does not work. Please, what am I?

150. Fingers Absent

I follow you around all the time even though I once resided in one place. My fingers may be absent, but I have a ring. Please tell me what I am.

Chapter 3: Easy Tricky Riddles

1. Who Am I?

    I am your uncle's sister-in-law and your dad's better half.
    Who am I?

2. If I state, "Everything I say to you is a lie," is this statement a
    truthful one or a deceitful lie?

3. Before You Can Get It

    What is one thing that is taken before you can get it?

4. The Last Brick

    To complete one 10-story building made of bricks, how many
    bricks do you need?

5. Which One

    Phil enjoys tomatoes but hates potatoes. Phil enjoys peas but
    hates cabbage. Phil enjoys fresh squash but hates onions.
    Based on Phil's logic of liking the aforementioned, will Phil
    enjoy oranges or pumpkins?

6. Lucy, the Pet Shop Owner

   Lucy is a pet shop owner who keeps one parrot in a cage with the following signage: "This parrot repeats everything it hears." Someone bought the parrot, but the parrot never said anything back, for two full weeks. The person bought it back, but Lucy said she did not lie about the parrot. How can this be true?

7. Rita Is Trapped

   Rita's enclosed in a room with two ways to leave. A fire-breathing dragon is at the first door. The second way requires you to go through a magnifying glass that will burn you to death if you go through it. Rita is able to get out of the room. How does she do it?

8. Three Different Bags

   Two total marbles are in three separate bags. The first bag has a total of two marbles that are blue. The second bag has a total of two marbles that are green. The third bag has a total of two marbles, but one marble is green, and the other marble is blue. You pick one of the bags randomly and take out a total of one marble that is blue. What is the probability that the remaining marble from the same bag is also blue?

9. A Man on the 11th Floor

   Every day after working on the 11th floor all day, a man takes the elevator to the first floor. However, on the way to work each morning, he takes the elevator up to the 8th floor and then uses the stairs to arrive at the 11th floor, no matter what, unless his colleagues are on the elevator with him or it's raining outside. Explain why he does this.

10. Caught

   After trespassing on the King's hunting property, a person is caught. "You must give me a statement. If the statement is true, you will be killed by lions. If the statement is false, you will be killed by trampling of wild buffalo," the King tells him. After his statement, the man is released. What did the man say to save his life?

11. Traveling the Sea

   How can two sailors standing on opposite sides of the ship, one in the western direction and the other in the eastern direction, still see each other clearly?

12. At an Animal Show

   Recently at an animal show, all of the participants were fish, except two. All of the participants were dogs except two. All of the participants were cats except two. What number of participants are fish, cats, and dogs?

13. No Red Eyes

No red eyes are allowed in the monastery full of silent monks. The monastery contains no mirrors. If a monk realizes he has eyes that are red, he must leave immediately. Everyone is okay until someone visits the monastery and states that one monk has eyes that are red. What is the next part of this story?

14. A Fishing Trip

A fishing trip consists of sons and two dads. Each father and child caught one fish. After arriving at the shore, a total of three fish were in the boat and none of the fish was eaten, thrown into the water, or randomly lost. Explain how this happens.

15. Five Bolts

Five bolts exist in a row and they are all connected to each other. The first bolt goes in a clockwise direction. In which direction is the fifth bolt turning?

Chapter 4: Hard Tricky Riddles

1. An Island Is Burning

    An island with a forest is burning, and a woman is stranded there. The fire starts on the west side of the island and is quickly burning. There is no way for the woman to put the fire out. She has no hoses or buckets that she can use. She cannot even jump off the island because jagged rocks surround it. If she would jump, it would be certain death. How can she survive?

2. An Intersection

    There is a fork at the road, and you are standing there. In the first direction lies the City of Truth, and the other direction lies the City of Lies. Citizens of the City of Lies always tell lies. Citizens of the City of Truth always tell the truth. A citizen of one of those cities is at the intersection. You have no idea what city the person is from, but you need to ask for help, so you can get to the right place. What is the one question you could ask this person to find out the way to the City of Truth?

3. Friends and Apples

    Ten apples are in a basket that you have. All ten of your friends want one. You give every friend one apple because you are a very nice person. All your friends thank you for your kindness. Now every friend has an apple, but there is still an apple in the basket. Explain the way this is possible. Think hard, but don't think too long.

4. A Knave, a Knight, and a Spy

    There are three people, (Al, Ben, and Cory), and one of the three people is a knave, a spy, and a knight. The knave always tells lies, the knight always tells the truth, and truth or a lie is what the spy can tell. Al states, "Cody is a knave." Ben states, "Alex is a knight." Cory states, "I am the spy." Figure out who is the knight, knave, and spy.

5. Two Children

    Two children, one boy and one girl, are talking. "I am a boy," said black-haired kid. "I am a girl," said the white-haired kid. A minimum of one of the kids did not tell the truth. Which child is the boy and which child is the girl?

6. Four Traveling People

    Four people are going various places using various modes of transportation. Rain, Joy, Mr. Johnson, and Candy are their names. The people used train, ship, plane or car. Mr. Johnson hates flying. Candy rents her transportation, and Joy becomes seasick. How did each of them travel?

7. Four More People

   Four more people, Amy, Benton, Cody, and Dennis must cross a stream in a boat. However, the boat carries only 100 pounds, or it will tip over. Amy weighs 90 pounds, Benton weight 80 pounds, Cory weighs 60 pounds and Dennis weighs 40 pounds. They also have 20 pounds of supplies. How do they get across the river?

8. Working at a Fruit Factory

   You see three crates in front of you while on your shift at a factory that produces fruit. The first crate has oranges only. The second crate has apples only. The last crate has a mixture of oranges and apples. However, the machine that does labels is not labeling boxes correctly. The mechanic at your factory is out on vacation so there is no one there to fix the machine. Deliveries still must go on, so you have to figure out what is in what crate. If you are only able to take out one piece of fruit from each crate, how are you able to label all of the boxes correctly?

9. Cannibals

Cannibals in a jungle capture three men. The cannibals will allow the men one chance to get away without being eaten up. The cannibals put the men they captured in a straight line according to their height. The tallest man sees the backs of his two friends. The man in the middle can only see the shortest man's back, and the shortest man cannot see anyone's back. The cannibals give all men the chance to look at five hats of which three are black and two are white. Two hats are white, and three hats are black. The cannibals then cover the men's eyes with blindfolds and put a random hat on the head of every man. The two remaining hats are hidden. The cannibals take the blindfold off and tell the men that if just one can guess what color of hat they are wearing on their head, they can all leave safely. The tallest man in the back says that he cannot guess. The man in the middle says that he cannot also guess. The man in the front says that he knows what hat he is wearing. How so?

10. Forgot Your Socks

You are about to go on a trip, but you forgot your socks. You hurry back up the stairs and rush into your room, but the electricity is off, so you are not able to see any of the colors of your socks. You aren't too worried, because you remember that in your sock baskets, there are a total of 10 pairs of socks that are yellow and ten pairs of socks that are green, and eleven pairs of pink socks, but they are all mixed up. You need to hurry and just grab some socks before you miss your airplane. You paid a lot for your ticket and will not get a refund for a missed flight. How many socks should you put in your bag to assure that at least one pair of the socks is matching?

Chapter 5: Super Easy and Hard Riddles — "What Am I?" Answers

Super Easy Riddles — "What Am I?" Answers

1. Drier, Yet Wetter

Answer: A towel.

2. 3 Miles Away

Answer: The horizon

3. Single Eye

Answer: A needle

4. Black Water

Answer: A lobster

5. Light as a Feather

Answer: Your breath

6. Oceans with No Water

Answer: A Map

7. Two Legs

Answer: A pair of pants

8. Like Bacon and An Egg

Answer: A snake

9. Easy to Get Into

Answer: Trouble

10. Clap and Rumble

Answer: Thunder

11. Neck and No Head

Answer: A bottle

12. Big Bark

Answer: A tree

13. Smooth or Rough Jacket

Answer: A book

14. Up and Down

Answer: A staircase

15. Fly All Day

Answer: A flag

16. Wet Coat

Answer: A coat of paint

17. Unwinnable Bet

Answer: The alphabet

18. Unwearable Dress

Answer: Your address

19. Eyes That Cannot See

Answer: A shoe

20. Serve But Not Eaten

Answer: A tennis ball

21. Limbs, But Cannot Walk

Answer: A tree

22. Come Down But Not Up

Answer: Rain

23. Beat with No Cries

Answer: An egg

24. Travel in One Spot

Answer: A stamp

25. Catch

Answer: A cold

26. Four Eyes

Answer: Mississippi

27. Eighty-eight Keys

Answer: A piano

28. Always Coming

Answer: Tomorrow

29. Careful, Fragile

Answer: A promise

30. Round on Both Sides

Answer: Ohio

31. Lose My Head

Answer: A pillow

32. Hear, But No Body

Answer: Your Voice

33. Rich and Poor People

Answer: Nothing

34. Don't Share

Answer: A secret

35. The More You Take

Answer: A hole

36. Born in the Air

Answer: An echo

37. Millions of Years

Answer: The moon

38. Give It Away

Answer: Your word

39. Stand on One Leg

Answer: A cabbage

40. You Can Throw Me Away

Answer: Corn on the cob

41. Used for Light

Answer: A window

42. Higher Without the Head

Answer: A pillow

43. If I Drink

A fire is the answer.

44. First Letter is Gone

Answer: Empty

45. No Bones or Legs

Answer: An egg

46. Tall When Young

Answer: A candle

47. Throw Me Away

Answer: An anchor

48. When Water Comes

Answer: An umbrella

49. The Maker Doesn't Need Me

Answer: A coffin

50. People Need Me to Eat

Answer: A plate

51. Many Times

Answer: Footsteps

52. End of the Rainbow

Answer: Water

53. Never Ask Questions

Answer: The doorbell

54. No Life

Answer: A battery

55. I Have A Mouth

Answer: A River

56. Lots of Memories

Answer: A photo frame

57. I Go Around and Around

Answer: A street

58. Flying Without Wings

Answer: A cloud

59. No Senses, But I Sense

Answer: A brain

60. Wrong Word

Answer: The word 'wrong'

61. Keys But No Locks

Answer: Keyboard

62. You Take Me

Answer: A pencil

63. Backwards Cheese

Answer: Edam

64. Lots of Letters

Answer: A Post Office

65. A Type of Ship

Answer: A relationship

66. A Mini Tree

Answer: A palm

67. Super Delicate

Answer: Silence

68. One Head, Not Human

Answer: A bed

69. Everyone Needs Me

Answer: Advice

70. What Word

Answer: Shorter

71. A Vehicle

Answer: Racecar

72. What State

Answer: Hawaii

73. Every Night

Answer: Stars

74. Middle of Gravity

The letter 'v' is the answer.

75. Just A Fruit

Answer: Pear

76. No Flaky Hair

Answer: Corn

77. Pilgrim Music

Answer: Plymouth Rock

78. Dangerous

Answer: Words

79. A Man's Weakness

Answer: Sleep

80. I Belong to You

Answer: Your Name

81. I Can Be Long or Short

Answer: A fingernail

82. I Have Just One

Answer: A cat

83. Men and Women

Answer: Music

84. Container with No Hinges

Answer: An egg

85. One Color

Answer: A shadow

86. Reach for the Sky

Answer: A tree

87. I Have Three Letters

Answer: Eye

88. Sometimes White, Sometimes Black

Answer: A hearse

89. Red or Green

Answer: Peppers

90. Many Legs

Answer: A broom

91. An Insect

Answer: Beetle

92. Many Feathers

Answer: An arrow

93. A Potato's Tool

Answer: A TV remote control

94. No Lungs

Answer: Fire

95. First in the Ocean

Answer: An owl

96. Very Skinny

Answer: A tornado

97. Invisible, Yet There

Answer: A soul

98. Slim and Tall

Answer: A cigarette

99. To Measure or Not to Measure

Answer: Time

100. White and Grind
Answer: Teeth

101. Walk on Four Legs
Answer: Man

102. Cannot Control Me
Answer: A baby

103. Can't Catch Me
Answer: Wind

104. One Blind Eye
Answer: A hurricane

105. Different Colors
Answer: Charcoal

106. Pointed Teeth
Answer: A stapler

107. No eyes
Answer: A skull

108. Weight in My Belly

Answer: A ship

109. Cannot Be Seen

Answer: Darkness

110. Light and Hidden

Answer: An iceberg

111. Between Your Head and Toes

Answer: A bar of soap

112. Different Sizes and Shapes

Answer: A jigsaw puzzle piece

113. Sleep in The Day

Answer: A bat

114. Travel Low and High

Answer: Musical Notes

115. None Seeps

Answer: Your skin

116. Thirty Men

Answer: A chess match

117. Often Held

Answer: A person's tongue

118. Up and Down

Answer: A see-saw

119. Tear Me Off

Answer: Matches

120. No Fingers

Answer: A wheelbarrow

121. Crack A Smile

Answer: A mirror

122. Always Old

Answer: The Moon

123. Loud Noise

Answer: Popcorn

124. You Hear

Answer: An echo

125. What Letter
Answer: The letter 'R'

126. Ruler of Shovels
Answer: The King from the Spades suite

127. Four Fingers
Answer: A glove

128. The Pope Does Not Use It
Answer: A last name

129. Invisible Roots
Answer: A mountain

130. Nothing on the Outside
Answer: A bubble

131. Beauty in the Sky
Answer: A rainbow

132. No Drinks from This Fountain
Answer: Oil

133. A Precious Stone

Answer: Ice

134. I Beam

Answer: A smile

135. I Devour

Answer: Time

136. I Am Small

Answer: A hummingbird

137. I Am Big

Answer: An elephant

138. I March Before Armies

Answer: A flag

139. Start of All Ideas

Answer: Paper

140. My Children

Answer: Sun

141. I Can Fall

Answer: Water

142. Stop and Look

Answer: Horizon

143. You Have Me

Answer: Memories

144. In You

Answer: Water

145. Cracked

Answer: A joke

146. I Am Red

Answer: A heart

147. Sweet Rest

Answer: A pillow

148. Soup or Burger

Answer: A tomato

149. Children Love Me

Answer: A kite

150. The Ocean Is My Hand

Answer: A fish

151. Don't Drop Me

Answer: A cellphone

152. I Wiggle

Answer: A worm

153. A Special Room

Answer: A mushroom

154. Wave Me

Answer: A fan

155. Three Eyes

Answer: A traffic light

156. Forward and Backward

Answer: A rocking chair

157. Long Tail

Answer: A mouse

158. Carry Me

Answer: An umbrella

159. No Voice

Answer: A book

160. Different Colors

Answer: Flowers

161. Bigger When Full

Answer: A balloon

162. Brick Body

Answer: A house

163. Keep Me Away

Answer: Scissors

164. Easily Overlooked

Answer: A nose

165. The Harder You Run

Answer: Your breath

166. Twirl My Body

Answer: A screw

167. Seed

Answer: A pea

168. Going Up

Answer: Your age

169. Green Jacket

Answer: Watermelon

170. Black as Night

Answer: A bowling ball

171. Good at Hiding

Answer: Makeup

172. Pure, But Forgotten

Answer: Air

173. I Ran

Answer: An Hourglass

174. A Mother

Answer: Earth

175. Never Stolen

Answer: Knowledge

176. Enjoyed by Some

Answer: Marriage

177. Soft and Hairy

Answer: Carpet

178. A Ring

Answer: Telephone

179. Take Off My Clothes

Answer: A clothes hanger

180. Metal or Bone

Answer: A comb

181. Run Around

Answer: A shoe

182. The Protector

Answer: Sunglasses

183. An Absolute Necessity

Answer: Coffee

184. Not Born
Answer: A clone

185. In the Rainforest
Answer: A sloth

186. Buttons or a Zipper
Answer: A coat

187. Jump and Climb
Answer: A spider

188. Go Up
Answer: A ball

189. Keep You Entertained
Answer: A television

190. Curly and Bald
Answer: Hair

191. In the Woods
Answer: A splinter

192. Wake You

Answer: A rooster

193. Lick, Lick

Answer: Ice cream

194. A Fruit

Answer: A date

195. Two Meanings

Answer: A tie

196. A Food

Answer: Wheat

197. I Am Scary

Answer: Smoke

198. A Small Piece of Paper

Answer: A ticket

199. Can Be Embarrassing

Answer: Scale

200. People Walk in Me

Answer: An elevator

Hard "What Am I?" Riddle Answers

1. Beginning of the End

Answer: The letter 'e' is the first letter of 'end' and the last letter of 'place.' 'E' also is the first letter of 'eternity' and the last letter of the words 'space' and 'time.'

2. First

Answer: A badger

3. Creature of Power

Answer: Tree

4. Two Sisters

Answer: Salt and pepper

5. Four-Letter Word

Answer: Noon

6. The Traveling Letter

Answer: T

7. Covered in White

Answer: Frost

8. White and Dirty

Answer: A chalkboard

9. Hard Tongue

Answer: A bell

10. Letters Equal to Six

Answer: Member

11. Three Lives

Answer: Water

12. Sky and the Ground

Answer: Leaf

13. Fall and Break

Answer: Day and Night

14.Water of Life

Answer: Blood

15. Forward

Answer: Ton

16. Feel Me, But Can't See
Answer: Your fears

17. Bat with Me
Answer: Eyelashes

18. Red Tears
Answer: A cherry

19. Use Me Everyday
Answer: Your feet

20. Creative Memories
Answer: Music

21. Served at a Table
Answer: Ping pong balls

22. Out the Earth
Answer: An onion

23. Dog's Name
Answer: K9

24. Straight Through Me

Answer: The blink of an eye

25. I Am Not Magic

Answer: Mirror

26. Share, But Selfish

Answer: Knowledge

27. I Am Two

Answer: The letter 'r'

28. Thunder Before Lightning

Answer: A volcano

29. Five and Six

Answer: A clock

30. Give Me Away

Answer: Money

31. Starts with Gas

Answer: An automobile

32. Shave Beards

Answer: A barber

33. Hides at Night

Answer: A fly

34. There Is a Word

Answer: Heroine

35. In the Past

Answer: History

36. See Me in Water

Answer: A reflection

37. My Brother

Answer: Thunder and lightning

38. I Travel Alone

Answer: A shadow

39. Summertime Favorite

Answer: A marshmallow

40. Sweet or Sour

Answer: Orange

41. Compliments People
Answer: Hand

42. A Simple Circle
Answer: Zero

43. Two in a Whole
Answer: Half

44. Digging a Tiny Cave
Answer: A dentist

45. Simple or Complex
Answer: A pattern

46. Some People
Answer: Calories

47. It May Sound
Answer: A busboy

48. A Shimmering Field
Answer: Ocean

49. Write on Me

Answer: A floppy disk

50. Folding

Answer: A Paper Cut

51. Two Occupants

Answer: A peanut

52. Walking and Running

Answer: A treadmill

53. Not My Name

Answer: Tombstone

54. In Window

Answer: Dove

55. You Can't Hide

Answer: Death

56. I Am Brown

Answer: A saddle

57. The Path

Answer: A valley

58. Once A God

Answer: A cat

59. Soft Like Silk

Answer: Cotton

60. Two-faced

Answer: A coin

61. Very Tempting

Answer: An apple

62. When Young

Answer: Wine

63. My Title

Answer: A knight

64. Head Bob

Answer: A daisy

65. Perfect with a Head

Answer: A wig

66. Add the Letter S
Answer: Dice

67. More Shoes
Answer: The ground

68. Your Mechanic's Name
Answer: Will

69. Beneath Your Roof
Answer: Wood

70. Cut Through Evil
Answer: Justice

71. I Have Two
Answer: Sharing

72. Something Sweet
Answer: Kitchen

73. Busy Street
Answer: Parking meter

74. I Heard of a Wonder

Answer: A bookworm

75. Moving Slow

Answer: Your hair

76. Take a Spin

Answer: A Fan

77. Bury Me

Answer: A plant

78. I Can Help You See

Answer: Sand

79. Born of Water

Answer: A mosquito

80. Everyone Faces Me

Answer: A birthday

81. Silver-tongued

Answer: Mercury (This element of the periodic table looks wet, shiny, and silver. Also, the god Mercy has two wings but only uses them to run.)

82. Twelve Is Left
Answer: Dozens

83. White Father, Black Child
Answer: Smoke

84. Alive Without A Breath
Answer: Fish

85. Visible to You
Answer: Time

86. Speak the Truth
Answer: A book

87. Airy Creatures
Answer: Vowels

88. Peep, Peep
Answer: A star

89. A Utensil

Answer: A knife

90. A Hundred Years

Answer: A tree

91. Helping Engines

Answer: A belt

92. They Belong to Me

Answer: Thoughts

93. I Am Round

Answer: Football

94. Beautiful and Cold

Answer: A vampire

95. Lovely and Round

Answer: A pear

96. End of My Yard

Answer: Flax

97. Makes No Sense

Answer: Dreams

98. First a Blessing

Answer: A rainbow

99. Used for Light

Answer: A window

100. Backbite

Answer: A flea

101. I Can Wave

Answer: An electric fan

102. Forest Without Trees

Answer: The zoo

103. Heavy Feet

Answer: The gallows

104. Sleeping During the Day

Answer: Sunrise

105. Lacking Reason

Answer: A Riddle

106. I Drink

Answer: A pen

107. A Tradition

Answer: Alchemy

108. Small and Light

Answer: A lighter

109. Four Legs

Answer: A desk

110. Every Dawn

Answer: The letter 'D'

111. Only the Maker

Answer: A promise

112. A Delectable Thing

Answer: A kiss

113. In a Box

Answer: Jewel

114. Moved and Rolled

Answer: A ball

115. Left or Right

Answer: A thumb

116. A Staple Food

Answer: Rice

117. Four Wings

Answer: A windmill

118. First in Family

Answer: Fruit

119. Softly Tread

Answer: Stairs

120. I Am A Tool

Answer: A pen

121. Shifting Around

Answer: A tectonic plate

122. Women

Answer: A baby

123. Ancient

Answer: Pyramids

124. Glitters

Answer: Rock

125. Don't Breathe

Answer: Leg

126. Known to Be Deceitful

Answer: Snake

127. More Than Life

Answer: Nothing

128. Caught in My Trap

Answer: A mirror

129. In Wealth

Answer: A bank

130. First Master

Answer: Fur

131. Weird Creature

Answer: A train

132. Bleed Without Blood

Answer: Wood

133. Tender Voice

Answer: Violin

134. A Slippery Fish

Answer: Soap

135. My Love

Answer: Moon

136. In My Entirety

Answer: A stable

137. Two Little Brothers

Answer: Dice

138. Soft and Cuddly

Answer: A teddy bear

139. I Catch Warmth

Answer: Clouds

140. Open Barrel
Answer: A thimble

141. Keep Things Green
Answer: A sprinkler

142. Red Liquid
Answer: Blood bank

143. Whoever Makes Me
Answer: Poison

144. Empty Inside
Answer: A pen

145. English Word
Answer: Bookkeeper

146. Two Eyes
Answer: A peacock

147. Flora
Answer: Bush

148. Turn Me Over

Answer: Odometer

149. Unique Teeth

Answer: A key

150. No Fingers

Answer: Telephone

Chapter 6: Tricky Riddles' Answers

Easy Tricky Riddles' Answers

1. Who Am I?

   Answer: Your mother

2. If

   Answer: A lie

3. Before You Can Get It

   Answer: A picture

4. How Many Bricks

   Answer: Just one. The 'last' brick completes the building.

5. Which One

   Answer: Pumpkins. Terry only likes foods that grow on vines.

6. Lucy, The Pet Shop Owner

   Answer: Lucy didn't lie because the parrot was deaf.

7. Rita Is Trapped

Answer: Rita escapes by waiting until night time and going through the second door.

8. Three Different Bags

    Answer: There is a 2/3 chance, not 1/2 chances. You know that you did not big from Bag B with the two green marbles, so you have three possibilities. You chose Bag A, first blue marble. The other marble will be blue. You chose Bag A, second blue marble. The other marble will be blue. You chose Bag C, the blue marble. So, the other marble will be green. So, 2 out of 3 possibilities are blue. The answer is not 1/2 because you are selecting marbles, not bags.

9. A Man on the 11th Floor

    Answer: The man is too short to reach the '20' button. However, when other people are on the elevator with him, he can ask them to push the button for the 2oth floor. On a rainy day, he has an umbrella, so he can push the button using that.

10. Caught

    Answer: "I will be killed by trampling of wild buffalo." The King is unable to say that is the correct answer because if that answer is true, the man will need to be killed by lions. But if the man is killed by the lions, then his answer is not the truth, and he will need to be stomped on by the buffalo. So, the king just let the man go.

11. Traveling the Sea

Answer: The sailors had their backs turned to either end of the ship.

12. At an Animal Show

Answer: There are only three total animals at the show — one dog, one cat, and one fish. If all the animals were there except for two, then that would satisfy the requirements of the riddle.

13. No Red Eyes

Answer: If there is only one monk with a red eye, he will see the monk and know he is the one with the eye that is red and will leave. If there are two, one will see the red eye and stay. If the second monk sees the man staying, the next morning, he will know that he has the red eye. So on and so forth.

14. A Fishing Trip

Answer: The trip consists of a total of three people: the son, father, and his grandfather.

15. Five Bolts

Answer: It is rotating clockwise.

Hard Tricky Riddles' Answers

1. A Burning Island

    Answer: The woman will quickly get a stick and set fire to the eastern side of the island. The wind will cause the fires to cancel each other out and she can stay in the burnt part until the fire is finished. However, even though she is capable of surviving the fire, she will die by starving because the fire will leave absolutely no food that she can eat. She also would not be able to drink the sea water. Worst-case scenario, she could drink her urine, but at some point, she would still be left with no food or a way to survive unless someone rescues her.

2. An Intersection

    Answer: You will ask, "What direction do you live?" A Citizen of the City of Truth will point to the City of Truth. A Citizen of the City of Lies will point to the City of Truth. From their answer, you will know which way to go in order to arrive at your destination.

3. Friends and Apples

    Answer: You gave an apple to the first nine friends, and then gave the apple in the basket to the last friend, thus the last apple in the basket is the apple of the tenth friend.

4. A Knave, A Knight, and a Spy

Answer: Al is a knight. Ben is a spy, and Cory is a knave. Ben is not the knight since if he was, Al would be the knight, too. Cory is not the knight since his statement would automatically be a lie. So, Al equals the knight. Cory equals the knave, and Ben equals the spy.

5. A Girl and a Boy

Answer: They both told a lie. The child with the black hair is the girl, and the child with the white hair is the boy. If only one of them lied, they would both be girls, or both would be boys.

6. Four Traveling People

Answer: There are three different possibilities.

1. Candy — car; Mr. Johnson — train; Joy — plane; Rain — ship
2. Candy — car; Mr. Johnson — ship; Joy — plane; Rain — train
3. Candy — car; Mr. Johnson — ship; Joy — train; Rain — plane

7. Four More People

Answer: Cody and Dennis row across; Dennis returns. Amy rows over and Cody returns. Cody and Dennis row across again, Dennis returns. Benton rows across with the supplies and Cody returns. Cody and Dennis row across again for the last time.

8. Working at a Fruit Factory

Answer: You should start by taking a piece of fruit from the crate that states 'oranges and apples.' If an apple is pulled out, then you know that it is the apples' crate since all the labels are not correct. So, the crate that states 'apples' must really be 'oranges' and the one marked 'oranges' must really be the 'oranges and apples' crate. If you pull out an orange, you will follow the same logic, just use the opposite of what was aforementioned.

9. Cannibals

Answer: The man at the front is wearing a black hat because he knows that the tallest man could not see hats that were all white. The middle man did not see a white hat, because if he would have seen a white hat, the middle man would have known that his hat was black from hearing what the first man said.

10. Forgot Your Socks

Answer: The correct answer is four. Although there are lots of socks in the drawer, there are only three colors, so if you take four socks, then you are assured to have one pair that matches.

Conclusion

Thanks for making it through to the end of *The King of Riddles*. Let's hope it was informative and able to provide you with all of the tools you need to achieve your goals whatever they may be. You may start to see amazing results from doing these riddles such as improving your thought process and how you feel when solving difficult problems. Don't fret! Just enjoy it.

The next step is to keep practicing in order to improve and enjoy the benefits of doing riddles. You can research for more riddles or even try your hand at creating riddles for all your family and friends to solve. You can even go back and review the riddles you found that were the trickiest in this book. Or you can challenge others with the riddles that were the hardest for you to see how they react. Whatever you do, just keep practicing. As the cliché says, "Practice makes perfect," and in this case, it is definitely true.

Finally, if you found this book useful in any way, a review on Amazon is always appreciated!

Catch us on Facebook www.facebook.com/bluesourceandfriends

Don't forget to claim your FREE book
https://tinyurl.com/karenbrainteasers

Karen J. Bun

45945894R00090

Made in the USA
Lexington, KY
20 July 2019